PRAYING WITH SAINT AUGUSTINE

Uniform with this volume
PRAYING WITH SAINT FRANCIS

Other titles in preparation

PRAYING WITH
Saint Augustine

Compiled by
Valeria Boldoni

Translated by
Paula Clifford

Introduction by Murray Watts

TRI△NGLE

First published 1987
Triangle
SPCK
Holy Trinity Church
Marylebone Road
London NW1 4DU

Selection copyright © 1984 Figlie di San Paolo, Rome, as
Signore, Dio di Verita. Translation and Introduction copyright
© 1987 The Society for Promoting Christian Knowledge

British Library Cataloguing in Publication Data

Augustine, *Saint, Bishop of Hippo*
    Praying with Saint Augustine.——(Praying
    with——).
    1. Prayer-books
    I. Title II. Signore dio di verita.
    English
    242'.8 BV245

    ISBN 0-281-04312-4

Printed and bound in Great Britain by
Hazell Watson & Viney Limited,
Member of the BPCC Group,
Aylesbury, Bucks

Contents

Translator's Note

This collection of Augustine's prayers, which was originally published in Italian, is in many respects more of an adaptation than a strict translation of the original Latin. In the extracts from the *Confessions* in particular, the compiler has tended at times to paraphrase or explain the original, and at times to make significant omissions. Those taken from other sources, however, follow the Latin much more closely. The result is a set of meditations or prayers which have a beauty all of their own.

In putting them into English I have tried to remain faithful to the Italian rather than the Latin in order to convey something of the language's poetry. More especially I have attempted to render them in such a way as to make them genuinely usable as meditations. Where there are clear biblical allusions I have adopted the language of modern translations, generally following the wording of the New International Version but drawing also on the Good News Bible where this seemed to fit the context better.

PAULA CLIFFORD

Introduction

The very idea of a 'saint' is a problem to many people. It suggests remoteness. Artists down the centuries have increased the distance by imagining that saints, when they pray, can be sure that the heavens will open, God will reveal himself in majesty and a shaft of gold will illuminate their ecstatic faces. These men and women, according to the popular myth, have an extraordinary ability in the spiritual realm. Kneeling in their humble cells, prayer seems easy and the divine love an automatic favour.

The story of Augustine blows away all such ridiculous stereotypes. What sanctity he had was born out of an immense personal struggle. He is not a saint to depress 'ordinary mortals' with his exceptional piety. In fact, he is unexceptional in so many ways: in his sexual anxieties; in his complex relationship with his mother and his past; in the fickleness that led him to toy with various religious ideas as a young man; in his passionate need for friendship and peace of mind. What made Augustine exceptional was the originality of his intellect applied with such honesty and warmth to the Christian faith.

Augustine's life story is a history of intellectual success but of moral failures and successive defeats for human pride. His message is that only out of failure can a life of spiritual freedom be born; and only out of the unexceptional stuff of humanity can beauty and truth be created by God's grace. Only because of his very similarity to us – not his saintliness – can we confidently learn to pray with Augustine.

Augustine was born in Thagaste (now Souk-Ahras in modern Algeria) in AD 354. It was a small town, ordinary and depressingly dull, far from the great coastal cities of ancient Numidia. His father, Patricius, was a minor government official, a cog in the enormous bureaucratic machine that stretched across the unwieldly Roman Empire. Patricius' life was lost in the pettifogging world of forms in triplicate, municipal taxes, by-laws, civil disputes. He was not an easy man, nor an inspiring father, from the little that we know, but he was dedicated to his son's education. He was a pagan, married to a Christian, Monica.

Monica was a remarkable woman, one of the most powerful, possessive and yet deeply spiritual mothers in the history of Christendom. Augustine has given us a unique portrait of her in his autobiography, the *Confessions*. Monica's Christianity was simple, direct, full of faith, the opposite of the intellectual self-doubt that tormented her brilliant son for so many years. Yet Monica had to learn patience and wisdom. She had to watch her son set out on a spiritual pilgrimage which was to challenge her possessiveness and transform her own understanding of God in the years to come.

Augustine proved his brilliance right from the beginning. He went to school at Madaura, nearby, and rapidly outgrew the restraints of the formal education he was offered. He was always a deeply emotional and intuitive thinker, totally unsuited to learning by rote. His parents recognised his potential and, in 369, he was obliged to spend a year at home, his studies interrupted, whilst his father raised money to send him to university. It was a year when he was plunged into adolescent crisis. 'The brambles of lust grew high over my head,' he wrote in the *Confessions*. It was hardly surprising. Thagaste, like many modern towns, had more of a line in bars and street corners than it did in libraries. It was a forum for young bodies rather than inquiring minds. Augustine's lifestyle alarmed his mother. She prayed for him night and day. She even managed to lead Patricius, not a very promising candidate, to baptism in his old age; but she had no luck with her son.

Augustine went up to the University of Carthage in 371. He compounded his folly, in his mother's eyes, by soon becoming involved in a powerful religious sect known as the Manichees. To Monica, it was quite simply a heresy, whereas to Augustine it was an attractive and philosophically appealing alternative to her primitive Christianity. Monica, now a widow, was infuriated. She banned Augustine from her home. Augustine was undeterred. He had his own life to live, and he had already reinforced his independence by taking a concubine, who bore him a son, Adeodatus, 'gift of God'.

In fact Augustine was behaving quite conventionally in his society, by taking a mistress whom he never intended to marry – even if with hindsight we might wish for an inspired exception to the rules. It is clear that he loved her (astonishingly, she is never named in the *Confessions*, perhaps because her memory was still painful to Augustine); he was faithful to her for fourteen years; but he was simply a man of his time in treating the relationship as dispensable in due course. Underneath, however, profound sexual guilt – a disquiet about the very act of conception – was fomenting in Augustine's mind and was to generate trouble in years to come: trouble not only in Augustine's theology, but in the succeeding centuries of the Catholic Church.

Carthage was an intoxicating contrast to Thagaste. It had the splendour of a capital city. It was a great seaport with continual traffic from Rome, bringing a merchandise of intellectual ideas as well as the trade of the Empire. The school of rhetoric was down by the quayside, and Augustine could debate the current philosophies of the day with the continual reminder of the world outside, clamouring for his attention. He was never to be an intellectual recluse. He was a man of the market-place. His Christian conversion would not propel him into the desert, but into the cities of North Africa.

Manicheism, which had so attracted Augustine, had found its way to Carthage from the East, and was now spread in a network of secret societies and hidden influences throughout the Empire. To modern eyes, the cult seems arcane, fantastic. It is hard to imagine what a thoroughgoing intellectual like Augustine would want with the peculiar rituals it encouraged, whilst it is easy to understand his later attraction to the stimulus of Greek philosophy. Augustine, however, was young and, like many students, eager to experiment with new ideas. He managed to effect an uneasy reconciliation between his worldly lifestyle and his status as a 'hearer' of the cultic doctrine. The extremism of the religion appealed to him. It was thorough, uncompromising. It seemed like a logical system. No doubt he would have understood the attraction that many extreme cults had for the generation of the 1960s, which had lost itself in self-indulgence and was seeking for a way out. Yet, typically, he was reluctant to go the whole distance. He cherished his intellectual independence. He dabbled in astrology, he toyed with various thinkers, he argued with his teachers, he read voraciously. Then a book came into his hands, the *Hortensius* of Cicero. It painted a picture, with such a felicity of style and depth of feeling, with such calm conviction, of the pursuit of wisdom, that Augustine took the first step in his intellectual conversion. He was inflamed with the love of wisdom. He wanted nothing but to know this wisdom for himself. Cicero's concept of wisdom would lead him, by the very absence of the name of Christ from the book, to search for the fountainhead of true Wisdom.

For several years Augustine pursued a career as a teacher, but his ambitions eventually led him to leave Carthage for Rome, in 383. Monica was beside herself with grief. She saw her irreligious son disappearing over the seas, quite beyond her grasp, and – as she was momentarily tempted to believe – beyond the reach of Christ himself. But her unshakeable conviction remained, supported by dreams and visions, and the promise of an elderly bishop that 'the son of so many tears' could not be lost. Augustine would come to Christ one day. As it happened, that day was not far off.

Augustine arrived in Rome, already disenchanted with the Manichees. However, the move proved to be an anticlimax. The great metropolis, not unlike Carthage, was peopled with boorish students who did not pay their fees on time, and Augustine was grateful for a spectacular career opportunity which gave him the chance to move again quickly. He was offered – probably through the Manichean network to which he was still loosely attached – the professorship of rhetoric in Milan.

The new post included the role of imperial orator at the court, which was then based in Milan. Augustine found himself at the beating heart of the Empire. He was a few steps away from high office, perhaps a governorship. Ironically, had he pursued this 'career', unconverted, his name might now be no more than a faint inscription on some shattered monument overgrown with weeds. Yet social reputation attracted him powerfully at this moment of intoxicating success. A young African, thirty-two years old, speaking with a pronounced provincial accent, highly proficient in Latin literature but never having mastered the Greek writers, less well educated than many of his peers, now stood at the open door of imperial privilege. It was a remarkable achievement. Yet Augustine was increasingly tormented in his search for wisdom. He was a master of rhetoric, an orator already showing greatness, but he felt empty within. The failure of Manicheism had left a gap.

Augustine's great childhood friend, Alypius, had joined him in Milan. He, too, had journeyed from the narrow-minded world of Thagaste, through the invigorating intellectual climate of Carthage. He, too, had grown in academic maturity whilst somehow sinking lower in his own spiritual pilgrimage. Conversations with Alypius, now a successful lawyer, can only have convinced Augustine that both of them were living shallow lives. There were sins that proved inescapable. The body, as the Manichees believed, was a prison but, sceptical of religious solutions, Augustine had thrown away an assortment of keys which did not fit.

It was in this quandary that Augustine first visited the church in Milan. He went out of professional interest. The bishop, Ambrose, was a fine orator. He was a society figure in Milan, not because of a glittering lifestyle, nor by pandering to the court, but rather the opposite. Ambrose had opposed the imperial will on several occasions. He had stood by his convictions and he was a very difficult man to unnerve. He had a cool, detached intellect that excited Augustine's admiration. In one man, it seemed, the very qualities that he longed for himself, were encapsulated. Ambrose was enormously well-read. He was a preacher with a memorable turn of phrase. He was an aristocrat, a man who had abandoned his career as a Roman governor to accept a bishopric foisted upon him by the admiring people. He was a prophetic figure who exuded the confidence of a divine calling. When Ambrose spoke, it was not a question of debate, so much as of oracle.

Augustine was awed by the man. He desperately wanted to discuss Christianity but Ambrose was too busy or too aloof. He was certainly not aware that the young orator in the court would one day be the most influential bishop in Christendom. Augustine had to content himself with the sermons which, in turn, led him increasingly to re-examine the Bible in the light of contemporary philosophy. Ambrose helped him to emphasise the spiritual, which superseded the literal, interpretation of many Old Testament passages. He was shown how the coming of Christ was prefigured in the prophets. He saw parables, signs, symbols, of the Eternal Wisdom seeking to express itself in the human context. Gradually, he was led to an understanding of the Incarnation which did not repel him – the very idea of God made flesh was abhorrent to the Manichees. Rather, he came to see that the *Logos* of St John's Gospel, the Word, could be made flesh without losing anything of the divine nature. On the contrary, it was humanity that was being taken up into the Divinity and transformed by the life of Christ.

The intellectual conversion of Augustine was a long process and its penultimate stage was the discovery of Platonic philosophy through the works of Plotinus and Porphyry. Ambrose had been deeply influenced by their writings and the current climate of thought (now referred to as 'Neo-Platonism') had helped to shape his theology. In Milan, Augustine had encountered a Christian church that was engaged in the highest level of intellectual investigation of the philosophies of the day. It was not a ghetto of simplistic piety, but part of an extraordinary renaissance of thought in the late Empire. Christians were in the intellectual vanguard of their generation. There was no hiding from the hard questions, such as the problem of the origin of evil, but an attempt to formulate a proper theological response. One of the translators of the works of Plotinus into Latin, an eminent man of letters, Victorinus, had recently created a stir by announcing his conversion to Christ. It was not a descent into irrationality, but the logical conclusion of his quest. The story of Victorinus' conversion had a profound effect on Augustine, as did his discovery of the Platonists, which came near to a mystical experience. His soul was bathed in 'the Light that true love knows'. (*Confessions* VII)

Augustine registered as a catechumen. Morally,

however, he fell desperately short. He chided himself for his failures to live a good life. He tried unsuccessfully to fight against his sensual nature. Ambrose, the one who inspired him to believe in Christ as the source of all wisdom, was celibate. This bothered Augustine. He could not understand how a man could be so self-sufficient. How could he make a choice, seemingly effortless, to abandon all sexual activity, when this was the very thing that Augustine felt dominated his personal life? Celibacy became more and more identified in his mind with commitment to Christ.

His mother's arrival in Milan both inspired him in his search for peace and certainty in the Catholic faith, and at the same time precipitated a domestic crisis. She had plans for a respectable marriage for her son, one that would be socially and religiously suitable, and she persuaded him to send his concubine back to Africa.

The unnamed woman left both her lover and her son in Italy, returning to Numidia with a courageous determination not to give herself to any other man and vowing herself to God. Augustine could not match this integrity. He could not even wait for marriage. He took another mistress and descended into the depths of self-hatred. The Platonists, though they had shown him the light, could not show him the 'way to love'. Their books did not speak of Christ. 'In them no one listens to the voice, the voice that says "Come to me all you that labour."' (*Confessions*, VII)

Augustine finally turned to the epistles of St Paul and found medicine for his spiritual sickness. Conversion came, at last, in the garden of his home in Milan, on August 28th, 386. A visitor from Africa told him the story of some young Christians who had suddenly abandoned their plans for marriage and given themselves wholly to God. Yet again, Augustine was thrown into an agony of bitter self-reproach. He knew Christ was calling him, but he saw, with devastating clarity, that his own will was utterly powerless. He could will his fists to beat the ground, but he could not will his own conversion. It was then that he heard the famous voice, a child, singing, 'Pick up and read, pick up and read.' Not knowing whether it was an angel from God, or simply a little boy or girl singing a nursery rhyme, he took it as a divine command. He seized the copy of the Scriptures that he had been reading in the garden, and read the very first passage that caught his eye: 'Not in revelling and drunkenness, not in lust and wantonness, not in quarrel and rivalries. Rather arm yourselves with the Lord Jesus Christ: spend no more thought on nature and nature's appetites' (Romans 13. 13, 14). 'In an instant,' he tells us, 'as I came to the end of the sentence, it was as though the light of confidence flooded into my heart and all the darkness of doubt was dispelled.' (*Confessions*, VIII)

The *Confessions*, which traces the story above, is one of the greatest spiritual classics of all time. It has had a profound influence on Western consciousness, not simply as a work of theological importance, but above all as a deeply moving, and very human, story. It is a uniquely Christian work, set apart from all literature that had gone before. Its masterly self-analysis makes it the ancestor of the modern novel. Its form, a direct address to God, makes it quite naturally the source of many of the prayers in this book.

The narrative of the *Confessions* ends with the death of Monica. Her last months on earth, in 387, were spent in blissful companionship with her son. She had lived to see him baptized a Christian. Now she could enter into the relationship of spiritual union that she had always wanted. Speaking of the mysteries of salvation, Augustine and Monica were carried away so far in their thoughts, one afternoon at the port of Ostia, that they seemed to touch heaven. They lost themselves, and all their troubles, in a mystical experience of the love of God. When

Monica died Augustine was deeply affected. Now he was on the threshold not only of spiritual but also of emotional maturity, as he sailed back to Africa.

When Augustine returned to Thagaste in 388, his dream was to found a kind of intellectual retreat, and for a few years he managed to do this with his son Adeodatus, Alypius and others. Death soon broke up this intimate circle, Adeodatus dying before he was twenty and Nebridius, a friend who became almost as close as Alypius, also dying tragically young. But, above all, it was the realities of church life in Africa that destroyed Augustine's dream and, in doing so, perhaps gave us his greatest writings and reflections, which were so often written to meet practical demands. Instead of becoming a recluse, Augustine found himself besieged by the congregation in Hippo whilst on a visit to found a monastery there, and (extraordinarily to modern eyes) kidnapped and forcibly ordained priest. The ageing bishop Valerius had his eye on a successor, and who better than the most brilliant young Christian in Africa?

The union of Christ and the soul, which Augustine had glimpsed so vividly in the company of Monica at Ostia, was like one of the fountains in the gardens of a Roman villa, compared to the muddy waters of controversy in Africa. Heavenly aspirations ran into headlong confrontation with the 'grey areas' of Christian conduct in a bitterly divided church. In every town and city of Numidia, Catholic and the schismatic Donatist Christians were opposed, priest against priest, bishop against bishop. The Donatist sect was theologically orthodox but convinced of its own spiritual purity. It was a holiness movement, driven forward by fervent nationalistic pride, and it resisted the 'corrupting' influence of the Roman Church.

Christ was all but forgotten, as terrorist groups called the Circumcellions roamed the countryside attacking Catholics and burning their churches; and many Catholics were prepared to respond in kind.

Augustine tried argument, debate, pamphleteering, even writing doggerel poems against the Donatist claims, but eventually he was persuaded to call for state coercion. It was this decision, sealed at the council of Carthage in 411, presided over by the Imperial Commissioner Marcellinus and dominated by the oratory of Augustine, that sealed the fate of the Donatists. The leaders were exiled, their property was confiscated, recusants faced heavy fines and the movement was effectively banned. The forcible repression of heresy had begun and Augustine, sadly, stands at the beginning of a long and doleful history of violent Christianity. His works have been quoted, and misquoted, down the ages to justify inquisitorial methods, although Augustine, himself, was not a violent man, and customarily was courteous to his intellectual and theological opponents.

Ironically, at the very time the Catholics were relying on the power of the state for their preservation, the state itself was beginning to collapse, and along with it, as it tottered and crumbled all around, went the confidence of many wealthy and influential Roman Christians. Rome was sacked by invading armies even before the Council of Carthage had taken place, and increasingly the tribes from the north swept across the empire. Augustine turned away from fighting rival churches – he increasingly turned away from the sphere of politics – and gave the full force of his intellectual might to fighting ideas that he considered to be dangerously mistaken.

He defended his views on Christianity in an epic work of twenty-two volumes, *The City of God*. Perhaps the impossibility of controlling outward events, as he and bishops like Alypius had once tried to do, had filled him with pessimism about human endeavour. Now he fixed his eyes on the Heavenly City. His book was already treasured in the libraries of Christians all over the civilised world, as his own world was literally collapsing about him.

By 430, when Augustine lay dying, the city of Hippo was surrounded by a besieging army. Hundreds of churches had been burned down, and many Christians, of all persuasions, had lost their lives. Augustine was writing against heresy to the last. Pelagius, a British monk, had argued that each human soul contained within itself the potential for perfect obedience to God. Augustine believed this to be a fundamental error. His own struggle towards conversion – the abject failure of his own will to offer any hope – had made him an intractable opponent of such optimistic humanism; and he was ready to fight his theological battles to the last, whilst the literal battles raged all around him. He organised all his writings into a library, cataloguing and amending his works. Then, as he lay dying, he recited the four penitential psalms which had been written in large letters on the walls of his simple cell. The nearer he came to God, as so often with the saints, the more he was obsessed with his own sinfulness. His last prayers, as his first, were born out of a profound need for the grace of God.

Murray Watts
Cardiff, 1987

The Writings of St Augustine

The whole of Augustine's life revolves around his extraordinary spiritual journey; God made of him the 'prototype' of a man who undergoes radical conversion to Christ. In this respect Augustine's works have the double value of involving us in the most intimate torment of his life, and also of leading us to contemplate the highest values of Christianity.

The following are some of his major works, according to their general subject. The list is by no means exhaustive.

AUTOBIOGRAPHICAL: The *Confessions* and the *Retractations*: these mark a new literary genre, combining a personal life story with the celebration and praise of the God of Truth, who is at the centre of the author's life.

DOGMATIC: These were to be the reference points for theological dogmatic investigation throughout the Middle Ages, beginning with his *On the Trinity*, a work in fifteen volumes written over a twenty-year period from 399 to 419; this still remains today a work of reference in any speculation on the mystery of the Trinity. It is subdivided into three parts; scriptural arguments, formulation of dogma, and speculation on the mystery of the Trinity with analogies found in created things.

PHILOSOPHICAL: The *Dialogues*, written in the period between his conversion and his ordination to the presbyterate, at Cassiciacum, Milan, Rome and Thagaste. Set in dialogue form, they follow typically philosophical patterns of arguments: beatitude, certainty, immorality, the existence of God, the size of the soul, freedom, evil.

APOLOGETIC: These include the famous *City of God* in twenty-two books, which is arguably Augustine's greatest work and the synthesis of his philosophical, political and theological thought. Written between 413 and 426, it develops the basic idea that divine providence guides history, in which two cities are intermingled, the one founded on the love of self and the other on the love of God. The work deals with the great human questions as to the meaning of history itself, its beginning and end, the problem of the existence of evil and the struggle between evil and good.

MORAL AND PASTORAL: Foremost among these is the *De catechizandis rudibus*, a handbook of catechetical instruction reflecting Augustine's pastoral care; it is rich in pedagogical insights.

EXEGETICAL: These vary as to form and content; note especially *On Christian Learning*, the basis for all medieval allegorical study and Scriptural interpretation; the *De Genesi ad Litteram* (twelve volumes) is classed among the major Augustinian works: it contains a comprehensive treatise on anthropology and the doctrine of simultaneous creation and seminal thought.

POLEMICAL: There are many Augustinian works of refutation arising out of the heresies that were raging at the time: against Manicheism, Donatism, Pelagianism, against Julian of Aeclanum, Arianism, Marcionism and heresies in general.

Among Augustine's other works we should note the Commentaries (on St John's Gospel, the first Epistle of John and the Psalms) and the Sermons, the fruit of Augustine's pastoral activity which lasted for almost forty years without interruption.

As a footnote to this formidable achievement we should not forget the Letters. We can see from the 276 letters collected that they contain various arguments arising out of pastoral needs and theological and exegetical reflection. Particularly noteworthy is letter 130, addressed to Proba, which is virtually a treatise on prayer.

Augustine's literary output was extraordinary and there is little to compare with it either in the Church Fathers or in world literature; his works were inspired by the desire of the believer, pastor, philosopher, exegete and theologian to use all his resources to preach and proclaim Christ, with a zeal that at times abandons the stylistic perfection which is typical of the professional rhetorician, in the interests of the immediacy of the message. Yet there is no shortage of examples of literary art and true poetry and this often finds its most vivid expression in the prayers.

PRAYING
TO MEET WITH GOD

Your face, Lord, I will seek,

Psalm 27.8 NIV

Seeking

Father,
I am seeking:
I am hesitant and uncertain,
but will you, O God,
watch over each step of mine
and guide me.

Confessions XI, 17

If you leave us
we die!

I have turned back to you
and ask you to give me the means to draw
close to you.
If you leave us
we die!
But you will not leave us
because you are wholly good
and do not let a sincere heart seek you
without finding you.
I sought you honestly
and it is you who have made me capable of
    seeking you like this.
Teach me, Father, to seek you.
Set me free from error
that in this quest
I may meet no one but you.
If I set my heart on you alone,
let me find you, my Father.
But if some desire for other things remains in
    me,
then cleanse me yourself
and set me in a position to see you . . .
So I entrust this body of mine to you,
good and wise Father.
I will ask for it
whatever you yourself suggest to me
at the right moment.
I want only to invoke your mighty love
that I might turn wholly to you,
and let nothing hold me back from drawing
    near to you.

Let me lead a life of moderation,
courage, justice and prudence,
that I may love and fully understand your
  wisdom;
make me worthy of your house,
that I might become an inhabitant of your
  kingdom,
which is the very height of happiness.

Seeking true happiness

How should I seek you, O Lord?
In seeking you, my God,
I am looking for life's true happiness.
I will seek you so that my soul might live,
since it is you who give the soul its life.

Confessions X, 20

Thirsty for God

Like a stag panting for the stream,
   so my soul longs for you, O God.
My soul is thirsty for the living God.
When shall I come to see the face of my God?
O fount of life, spring of living water,
when shall I leave the barren earth
with neither paths nor water,
to come to the waters of your sweetness,
to see your power and your glory
and quench my thirst
with the waters of your mercy?
I am thirsty,
O Lord, fount of life,
satisfy me
I am thirsty for the living God.
When will I come and stand
before you, O Lord?
Shall I ever see that day of joy and happiness,
that day made by the Lord,
when we are to exalt and rejoice in him?
O day of brightness that knows no evening,
on which the sun does not set,
when I shall hear the voice of praise,
the voice of exaltation and splendour.
Come and share the master's happiness,
enter into eternal joy
in the house of the Lord your God . . .
share in that joy without sadness,
which is eternal rejoicing, where everything
will be good and nothing evil,
everything that you wish,
and nothing that you do not wish,
where life will be full, sweet and lovely,

never being lost in oblivion:
where there will be no enemy
to harm you,
no false security,
but total safety
and certain peace,
peaceful tranquility,
joyous happiness and happy eternity,
blessed Three in One and One in Three,
divine unity and
blessed vision of the Godhead,
a vision that is the joy of my Lord.
O greatest joy,
joy that is above all joys,
when shall I share in you and see my Lord
who dwells in you?
We await the Saviour, the Lord Jesus Christ,
who will transform our lowly bodies
so that they will be like his glorious body.
We await the Lord's return from the wedding
so that he may lead us in peace to his own
marriage feast.
Come, Lord Jesus, do not delay.
Come, Lord Jesus, draw near to us in peace;
come, our Saviour,
come, desire of all peoples.
Show us your face and we shall be saved.

Book of the Soul's Soliloquies with God XXXV

Bring us back to you

O God of power,
  bring us back to you:
show us your mercy and we shall be saved.
Wherever I may turn away from you,
and however beautiful the things I cling to,
my human soul is wedded to sorrow.
Yet beautiful things would not exist
if they did not have their origins in you.
They have both life and death:
once born they live and grow
and come to maturity,
but no sooner do they mature
than they fade and die.
At the very moment of birth
and of reaching out towards existence,
they are hurrying still more swiftly
towards death.
Such is the limit
you have set upon them,
because they are but parts of that reality
which has no existence of itself,
being made up of mere fragments that fade
   away . . .
My soul must not cling to
the things of creation;
Instead it must sing your praises,
O God, the creator of all things.

Confessions IV, 10

Give me light

O Lord, the Word, O God, the Word,
you are the light and through you light
was made;
you are the way, the truth and the life,
and in you there is no darkness
nor error, vanity nor death;
light,
without whom there is only darkness,
way,
aside from whom there is only error,
truth,
without whom there is only vanity,
life,
without whom there is only death,
speak a word,
say, O Lord, Let there be light,
that I may see the light and avoid darkness,
see the way and avoid false steps,
see truth and avoid vanity,
see life and avoid death.

Give me light
O Lord, my light,
my splendour and my salvation,
my Lord whom I will praise,
my God whom I will honour,
My Father whom I will love,
my husband to whom alone I will consecrate
myself.
Give light,
O light,
to this blind servant of yours
who sits in darkness and in the shadow of death,

and guide his feet into the way of peace;
by your light I will enter the wonderful place
   of the tabernacle
and go into the house of the Lord,
with songs of praise and exaltation.

In truth praise is life
through which I shall draw near to you,
the way
by which I shall leave my path of error
and return to you, the way,
because you are the true way of life.

Book of the Soul's Soliloquies with God IV

Here is my heart

Here is my heart, O God,
here it is with all its secrets;
look into my thoughts,
O my hope,
and take away all my wrong feelings:
let my eyes ever be on you
and release my feet from the snare.

Confessions IV, 6

The depth of your love

If I choose to remember my past sins
and my unenlightened soul,
it is not out of any love for them
but because I want to love you, my God.
It is in order to know the depth of your love
that I recall the wickedness of my past.
In that bitter memory
my hope is to feel your sweetness,
a sweetness in which there is no deception,
only happiness and security;
so I seek to restore unity within me
in the wake of those inner wounds
which tore me apart
when I gave myself up to vain things
and turned away from you,
the one true God.

May I seek you, O Lord

Grant me, O Lord, to know and
    understand
whether I must first pray to you before I praise
    you,
or whether I must first know you before I
    pray.
Is it possible to pray without knowing you first?
Those who do not know you could be misled
into praying to others.
But what if to be known you have to be
    invoked?
How can people pray to one they have not
    believed in?
And how can they believe
in one of whom they have not heard?
Those who seek the Lord will praise him
because he who seeks him finds him,
and he who has found him
cannot help but sing his praises.
May I seek you, O Lord, as I call upon you,
and call on you as I believe in you,
because at last we have heard the good news
    of you.
My faith calls to you O Lord,
the faith that you have given me
and instilled in me,
through your Son made man,
and thanks to him
who has preached the good news of you to us.

Confessions I, 1B

Give me the strength to seek you

O Lord my God,
  my only hope,
hear me in your goodness:
grant that I may not stop seeking you when I
    am weary,
but seek your presence ever more fervently.
Give me the strength to seek you:
you allow yourself to be found
and inspire in me the hope of finding you
through an ever-increasing knowledge of you.
I lay before you my strength and my weakness:
preserve my strength and heal my weakness.
I lay before you
my learning and my ignorance;
where you open a door for me
welcome me as I go in,
and where one is closed
open it to me when I knock.
Let me always remember you,
understand you
and love you.
Increase your gifts in me
until in the end you transform me
into a new creation.

On the Trinity XV, 28

Knocking at your door

Could one man
        teach another man
who you are?
Could an angel explain it to another angel
or an angel to a man?
We must ask you for understanding
and seek it in you;
we must knock at your door:
only in this way
can we receive
and find,
as it is opened to us.

Confessions XIII, 38

Grant me the request of my heart

Grant me, Lord, the request of my heart:
for in truth it is your gift
that I should desire it.
Grant me this,
O Father, for truly you know how to give
good things to your children;
grant me this,
since I have tried to understand
but have found it too difficult for me
until you uncover the truth.
I beseech you in the name of Christ,
the most Holy One,
let nothing hinder me.
I too have believed
and so I dare to speak;
this is the hope
that I live for:
to gaze upon the beauty of the Lord.

Confessions XI, 22

Running to you in love

Stir us up, O Lord,
inflame our hearts and fill us with delight:
be to us both fire and sweetness:
teach us to run to you in love.
Is it not true that many turn to you
out of the depths of their blindness?
As they draw near to you
they are filled with that light of yours
which gives us the right
to become your children.

Confessions VIII, 4

I was so slow to love you

I was so slow to love you, Lord,
your age-old beauty is still as new to me:
I was so slow to love you!
You were within me,
yet I stayed outside
seeking you there;
in my ugliness I grabbed at
the beautiful things of your creation.
Already you were with me,
but I was still far from you.
The things of this world kept me away: I did
  not know then
that if they had not existed through you
they would not have existed at all.
Then you called me
and your cry overcame my deafness;
you shone out
and your light overcame my blindness;
you surrounded me with your fragrance
and I breathed it in,
so that now I yearn for more of you;
I tasted you
and now I am hungry and thirsty for you;
you touched me,
and now I burn with longing for your peace.

Confessions X, 27

Do not be afraid

Do not be afraid
to throw yourself on the Lord!
He will not draw back
and let you fall!
Put your worries aside and throw yourself on
  him:
he will welcome you
and heal you.

PRAYING
FOR GOD TO CHANGE
OUR LIVES

I will set out and go back to my father.

Luke 15.18 NIV

Out of your sight

I have examined my failings, O Lord,
and have called for your hand to save me.
Even in my spiritual weakness
I saw your splendour
and overwhelmed I said to myself:
Who can approach such glory?
Yet once again I have let myself
be driven back out of your sight.
You are the truth
who presides over all things,
but I in my greed,
while not wanting to lose you,
wanted at the same time to possess a lie . . .
And so I lost you,
because you do not allow us to possess you
alongside a lie.

Confessions X, 41

What am I to you?

What am I to you
that you should so want me to
love you
that you are troubled if I fail to do so,
and utter threats against me?
As if it were not already
cause for great sorrow not to love you!
Tell me, I pray you,
O merciful Lord God,
what you are to me!
Say to my soul:
I am your salvation.
Say it so that I may hear.
My heart is ready, Lord,
to heed you:
open my heart and say to my soul:
I am your salvation.
I will hurry after that voice and thus be
reunited with you;
do not turn your face away from me:
since not to see it
would be death indeed.
My soul's dwelling place is too confined
for you to enter:
make it larger, I pray.
It is in ruins:
restore it, I pray.
It contains things contrary to your will:
I know and admit that,
but who can make it clean?
And to whom shall I cry if not to you?
Cleanse me, O Lord, of my secret sin,
and spare your servant from the sins of others.

I believe, and that is why I speak to you,
 O Lord,
as you already know.

The day of the Lord

How different are my days
from the days of the Lord!
They are 'my' days
because I took them for myself,
intoxicated as I was with my reckless
    independence
which led me to abandon him;
but since he is everywhere,
all powerful and ever present,
I fully deserved to be imprisoned
in the darkness of ignorance
and to bear on my feet the chains of mortality.
In these days of mine
I cried aloud:
'Free my soul from prison.'
And he brought me help –
his day of salvation.
He heard the prisoner in chains in his misery
and came to him.
In those days of mine that are past,
the sorrows of death surrounded me
and the dangers of hell were closing in on me:
they would not have come close to me
had I not strayed
so far away from you.
But they were so close as to have me in
    their grasp
and I did not see them,
because my joy was in the delights of the world.

Commentary on the Psalms

You are my comfort

Your constant love is better than life itself
and my life is as nothing;
this is why
your power has kept me safe
in my Lord, the Son of Man,
who mediates between you, the one true God,
    and all of us,
who go astray in the midst of material
    things
and live by them:
he gives me the means
to catch hold of him
who has already taken hold of me
and gathered me up
out of the emptiness of the past
to follow the one true God.
Thus forgetting the past
and without being distracted by the future
    which is destined to pass away,
I can move on towards the joy of your house –
the goal held out before me
on which I may concentrate wholeheartedly –
there I will hear songs of praise
and will gaze on your delights that never pass
    away.
Now is my time of weeping
and you, Lord, my eternal Father,
you are my comfort.
I am torn between past and future
in my ignorance of the mystery of time,
and my very thoughts
and the depth of my soul
are rent

by the tumult of change,
until I throw myself on you,
purified in the flames of your love.

Your servant

I am your servant,
O Lord,
your servant and the son of your maidservant.
You have freed me from my chains
and I will offer you a sacrifice of praise.
My heart and tongue will praise you
and every part of me will join in saying:
'Who can be like you, O Lord?'
They speak and you will answer,
saying to my soul:
I am your salvation.

Yet who am I?
What sort of person ?
I have done so much wrong!
If it was not my actions
it was my words,
and when it was not my words
it was my will!

But you, O Lord,
are good and compassionate:
your powerful hand
searches around in my inmost feelings, sunk
    in death,
and purifies the deep corruption
within my soul,
as the time comes when you no longer wish
    to see
what I previously desired,
when instead your will is what you wanted,
it is then that you purify me.
But where has my freedom been

for so long?
From what secret depths was it dragged out
in an instant
that I might agree to bow my head
beneath your yoke which is gentle
and accept on my shoulders your burden
    which is light,
O Lord Jesus Christ,
my strength and my redeemer?
How suddenly comforting it was
to lose the false comforts of the past !
I had long feared losing them,
and now it was a joy to throw them away.

Truly it was you who put them far from me,
my true and supreme comfort:
you put them far away
and set yourself in their place,
you who are sweeter than all pleasures,
brighter than all light,
more intimate than any secret
and more exalted than any honour,
except to those who exalt themselves.
Henceforth my soul will be free . . .
henceforth you will be my pleasure,
my greatness,
my richness and my Salvation,
O Lord my God.

Confessions IX, 1

Remove all falsehood

O Lord, my God,
hear my prayer:
in your mercy
answer my request;
it is not just for myself
but I make it too for my brothers in love;
you see into my heart and know that it is so.
Let me offer you my mind and my tongue
in your service,
if you will give me the means of making this
   offering.
I am poor and in need,
but you
richly bless all who call to you;
you who are free from care,
care for us.
Free my mouth and my heart
from all uncertainty and falsehood.

Confessions XI, 2

Give me life

Give me, O Lord, a heart that thinks on you;
a soul that delights in you,
a mind that contemplates you,
an intellect that understands you,
and a reason that always remains faithful to you,
most sweet one,
and loves you wisely,
O most wise love.

O life through whom all things live,
you give me life and you are my life,
life through whom I live
and without whom I die;
life through whom I am brought back to life
and without whom I am lost,
life in whom I rejoice,
and without whom I am in torment;
sweet, lovely, life-giving life
who can never be forgotten.

I pray you, where are you, where shall I
    find you,
to die to myself and to live in you?

Be near to me in my heart and my soul,
be in my mouth,
be near to help me as I languish,
languish out of love,
because without you I die
and thinking of you I come back to life again.

Book of the Soul's Soliloquies with God I

You know me

You know me,
  O God,
and I will know you as you know me.
O strength of my soul,
come into my soul and give it your likeness,
that you may possess it without spot or
    wrinkle.
This is my hope,
and it is why I speak and where I find joy . . .
You loved truth
because whoever lives by the truth
comes into the light;
I want to serve truth,
as I have confessed
both deep within my heart
in your presence,
and also in writing in front of many
    witnesses.
And even if I were to tell you nothing,
what part of me
could remain hidden from you,
O Lord,
whose eyes penetrate the depths
of human conscience?
I could never hide from you
even if I concealed your existence from myself!
But now my lament shows
how I am displeasing to myself,
and how pleasant instead is your resplendent
    presence,
how much I love and want you,
to the extent that I despise myself and push
    self aside

in order to choose you;
and it is only in matters concerning you
that I seek to please both myself and you,
O Lord, you who know what I am.

When they turn away from you

What offences can men commit against you,
O incorruptible God?
Who can sin against you,
since you cannot be harmed?
You punish men for what they do
to themselves
when they sin against you, truly
they are damaging their own lives . . .

O fount of life,
the one true creator and preserver of the universe;
because of their personal pride
men love only a part of you,
a false image.

Then they return to you in humility,
and you cleanse them of their wicked ways:
be indulgent
towards those who acknowledge their sins,
hear the cry of those
whose feet are fettered,
and free us from the chains
that we ourselves have made to bind us;
then we will no longer raise our heads against
    you,
and strike a pose of illusory freedom,
greedy for more possessions
at the risk of losing everything:
no longer will we put our own wellbeing first,
before you, the universal good.

Confessions III, 8

35

Seek peace

Remember this and take it to heart
you who are far from God,
surrender to the God who created you.
Remain faithful to him
and you will be saved;
rest in him and you will have peace.
Where do you want to go?
Are you seeking suffering?
Where will you go?
The good you long for
comes from him . . .
Why wander along painful and difficult paths?
Peace is not where you seek it!
You may seek it if you wish,
but that is not where you will find it.
You seek a happy life
in a place of death:
that cannot be!
How could there be a happy life
where there is no life at all?
Our life, the true life,
came down from above;
he took our death upon himself
to put an end to it
through the superabundance of his own life:
he let his summons ring out
so that we might rise up from below to be with him
in that inaccessible place
from whence he came to us;
he entered first into a virgin's womb

and took on human nature,
to join with our mortal flesh
and make it immortal;
and from there,
like a bridegroom leaving the bridal chamber,
he made haste to take his chosen path
with an enormous, joyful leap.
Indeed he did not linger,
but ran,
summoning us with his words and actions,
through his own life and death,
to turn to him:
that was why he came
and why he returned to heaven,
vanishing from our sight,
so that we might turn to find him
in our inmost hearts.
It is true that he went away,
yet he is still here.
He did not want to stay too long with us,
but he has never left us.

To the Trinity

O three coequal and coeternal Persons,
true and living God,
Father, Son and Holy Spirit,
who alone dwell in eternity in the light that is
hidden from us,
who created the earth by your power
and rule the whole universe with your wisdom,
holy, holy, holy God of Sabbaoth,
you are just and merciful,
wonderful, lovely and worthy of all praise;
only God, three persons in one single essence:
power, wisdom and goodness,
one and indivisible Trinity,
open the door of righteousness
when I knock;
when I enter I will praise the Lord.
See how I knock at your door
as a beggar, great Father.
Order it to be opened to anyone who knocks:
You said:
'Knock and it shall be opened'
O most merciful Father,
the tumultuous desires of my heart
and my weeping and wailing
wait outside your door.
Before you is all my longing
and my sighing is not hidden from you.
O Lord, do not hide your face from me,
do not turn your servant away in anger.
Father of all mercies,
hear my cry,
lay your hands on me
and pull me out of the deep waters,

out of the foul mud of the lake of misery;
let me not die
in your merciful sight,
but let me come close to you,
O Lord my God,
to see the richness of your kingdom
and your face ever before me,
and to sing praises to your holy name . . .
All praise, glory, merit, power,
splendour, blessedness and clemency
to God the Father,
God the Son
and God the Holy Spirit.

Book of the Soul's Soliloquies with God XXXVII

You made us for yourself

O Lord, you are great, you are to be highly
         praised;
Your power is great
and there are no limits to your wisdom.
And man, a tiny part
of your creative work,
wants to celebrate your praise,
man, who drags his own frailty behind him,
as a testimony to his sin
and to your desire to reject the proud;
in spite of this
a small part of your great work of creation
wants to celebrate your praise.
It is you who have aroused this desire in us
because you made us for yourself,
and our hearts will not be at peace
until they rest in you.

Confessions I, 1a

PRAYING
FOR GOD'S FORGIVENESS

His love is eternal.

Psalm 106.1 GNB

Hear me

Hear me, my Creator,
I am your creature
and I am lost;
I am your creature
and I am dying,
your creature
and reduced to nothing.
Your hands, O Lord,
made me and formed me,
those hands pierced with nails for me.
Do not despise, O Lord,
the work of your hands.
You have described me with your hand:
so read what you have written there and save me.
See, I sigh to you,
I your creature;
you are my creator,
recreate me;
see, I sigh to you,
I am your handiwork
and you are my life:
give me life.
Forgive me, O God,
for my days have no meaning.
I am ill
and call for healing.
I am blind
and hasten towards the light.
I am dead
and long for life.
You are healer, light and life.
Jesus of Nazareth have pity on me.
Son of David have pity on me.

O fount of mercy,
hear me crying out to you in my weakness.
Passing light,
hear him who is blind,
hold out your hand to him that he might come
    to you,
and in your light may see the light.
O living life,
call back to life him who is dead.

You have loved us so much

You have loved us so much, good Father!
You did not even keep back your own son,
but for our sake you gave him into the hands
  of the wicked.
You have loved us so much!
It was for us that he did not regard his
  equality with you
as a treasure to be coveted,
but became obedient to death,
even death on a cross!
He indeed,
who alone is free among the dead,
has the right to give up his own life
and the right to take it back again.
It is for our sake that he is both victor and victim
in your sight –
victor for the very reason that he was victim.
For our sake he is both priest and sacrifice
in your sight –
priest for the very reason that he was sacrifice.
He has saved your children from slavery:
he was born of you
and serves us.
It is for good reason that I place in him
my sure hope
that you, O my God,
will heal my every weakness,
through him who is at your right hand
pleading for us.
If it were not so
I should be overwhelmed by despair.

Confessions X, 43

He saved me

The Lord is merciful and just:
our God gives us his mercy.
He is merciful,
he is just and works mercy.
he has been merciful
above all because
he has inclined his ear to me;
and I would not have known
that he heard me
if I had not first heard the voice of his apostles
inviting me to cry out to him in my turn.
No one has ever called upon him
without first having been
called by him
That is why he is called merciful.
He is just because he metes out punishment,
and he is merciful because he draws us to himself.
He chastises all his sons
but welcomes them nonetheless;
and it is surely less bitter for me to be punished
than it is sweet to be restored in his love.
How could he not punish us
as he watches over our childhood
and prepares us to receive his inheritance
once we reach maturity?
What father does not chastise his sons?
I was humbled and he saved me.

Commentary on the Psalms

Make your son welcome

Now it is you alone that I love,
you alone that I follow,
you alone that I seek,
you alone that I feel ready to serve,
because you alone rule justly.
It is to your authority alone that I want to submit.
Command me, I pray, to do whatever you will,
but heal and open my ears
that I may hear your voice.
Heal and open my eyes
that I may see your will.
Drive out from me
all fickleness,
that I might acknowledge you alone.
Tell me where to look
that I may see you,
and I will place my hope in doing your will.
I beg you, make your son, a fugitive, welcome,
O God who are more loving than any father.
Let there be an end to what I have suffered
from my enemies
and put them under your feet;
let there be an end to the lies
through which they made me the object
of their derision.
Welcome now your servant
who fled far from them;
for they gave me a warm welcome
when as an outcast
I fled far from you,
and I feel that without you I would have to go back.
So open wide before me
the door on which I knock.

Teach me what I must do
to come near to you.
I have nothing
except my own good will.
All I know
is that what is changing and transitory
    deserves contempt,
and that we need to seek
what is unchanging and eternal.
I do this, Father,
because it is the only thing that now I know;
one thing I do not know
is how to draw nearer to you.
Inspire and guide me,
set a path before me.
If it is by faith that those
who seek refuge in you find you,
give me that faith;
if it is through strength,
give me that strength;
if it is through knowledge,
give me that knowledge.
Increase in me faith, hope and love.
How wonderful, how unique is your goodness!

Soliloquies I, 5

Hope in the Lord

'**O** God, where are you?'
I make the cry my own and thus I
find you.
I breathe in something of you
as I let my soul burst free within me
with shouts of praise and thanksgiving
and joyful sounds of celebration.
Yet my soul remains sorrowful
because it sinks back and becomes a dark abyss,
or rather because it knows it is ever a place of
darkness.
And so it is my faith,
which you kindled in the night
as a light to my path, which asks:
'Why are you so downcast, my soul?
Why are you so troubled?
Hope in the Lord:
his word will light your way.
Hope and keep on until the night,
mother of wretchedness, is over,
until the Lord's anger is spent;
for we too were once children of wrath,
walking in darkness.
We bear the marks of it within us,
in our bodies which are dead because of sin,
until at last morning breaks
and the darkness disappears.
Hope in the Lord.'

Confessions XIII, 14a

Setting us free

When we confess our wretchedness to you
and acknowledge your mercy to us,
we are revealing your love for us,
so that, as you have begun,
so you may complete the task of setting us free:
that we may cease to be unhappy
in ourselves
and become happy in you;
for you have called us
to become poor in spirit,
to be meek and to mourn,
to hunger and thirst for justice,
to be merciful, pure in heart
and authors of peace.

Confessions XI, 1

Take pity on me, O Lord!

When my whole being
   is united with you,
then I will feel no more sorrow or pain;
mine will be the true life
wholly filled by you.
You raise up all who are filled with your spirit;
but I am not yet so filled,
I am a burden to myself.
The worldly joys that I ought to lament
   struggle within me
with the sorrows in which I should rejoice,
and I do not know where the victory lies.
Take pity on me, O Lord,
for I am not hiding my wounds from you.
You are the doctor, I am the patient;
you are the giver of mercy – I am in great need
   of it.

Confessions X, 28

Rejoicing at repentance

Merciful Father,
   you rejoice more over one sinner who
   repents
than over ninety-nine righteous souls
who do not need to repent.
And so it is with great joy
that we hear the story
of the shepherd's happiness
as he brings back on his shoulders
the sheep that went astray,
and of the coin returned
to the treasury
while the neighbours celebrate with the woman
who found it;
and the rejoicing in your house
brings tears of joy
when the story is read
of the younger son
who died and came back to life,
who was lost and found again.
You rejoice in us and in your angels
made holy through your holy love;
you indeed are always the same,
never changing in your manner of being;
you know all those things
that do not last for ever
and that are not unchanging.

Confessions VIII, 3

You are everywhere

The wicked fled
so as not to see you watching them:
but then, being made blind,
they met with you
who never abandon
any part of your creation,
and were justly punished;
they sought escape from your goodness
and thus came face to face with your justice,
and were subject to your severe judgement.

They do not know that
you are everywhere,
and that no one place can contain you;
that you alone are present even to those
who run away from you.

Let them turn back, then,
and look for you,
since you do not desert your creatures
as they, for their part,
desert their Creator;
let them turn back
and see that you are there
in their hearts,
in the hearts of those who believe in you
and who give themselves up to you,
weeping on your breast
after a long and difficult journey.

You are ready to wipe away their tears
and then they weep still more,
but more gently,

because it is you, O Lord,
not some man of flesh and blood,
but you their Creator
who are there to restore and comfort them.

But when I sought you where was I?
You were before me,
but I had strayed far away
and could not even find myself;
much less could I find you.

God of mercy

Not even the heart which is the most
turned in on itself
can hide from your sight,
nor can man's hardness
put away your hand;
you can set a heart free just as you wish,
with your forgiveness or punishment.
Nothing can hide from your heat.
Let my soul praise you
and so reveal its love;
let it celebrate your mercies
and so reveal your greatness.
All that you have created
reveals it unceasingly:
mankind whom you created
looks to you in adoration,
as do all created things,
whether or not they have life,
through him who looks on them.
Thus our soul
depends for support on all creatures:
it is lifted up out of its weakness
and, thanks to them,
is joined with you,
their most wonderful creator.
And in you we are restored and find true strength.

Confessions V, 1

Enter my soul

I call upon you,
most merciful God,
who created me
and did not forget me
when I forgot you.
I call upon you to enter my soul
which you yourself prepared to receive you
through inspiring it with longing.
Do not desert the one who calls upon you:
you anticipated it
even before I called upon you,
as you insisted on summoning me
ever more loudly
in different ways,
so that I sensed you from afar
and turned to call upon you
who were summoning me.

You, O Lord,
have cancelled out all my sins
so as not to inflict punishment on these hands
which have failed you,
and you have taken account of my good points
so as to reward me with your hands
which created me;
indeed before I existed
you were already in existence;
but the reason I did not exist
was precisely so that
you might give me existence.

Now that I do exist
it is through your sheer goodness:
your goodness has gone before me
in all that I am
and by it I was made.

You did not need me,
nor am I an asset
which might be helpful to you,
my Lord and my God:
if I put myself at your disposal
you would not labour any less,
and your power would not be diminished
if by chance my praise were missing.
I cannot worship you
in the same way as I till the land,
so that if I do not cultivate you you remain
    untilled:
it is I who must serve you
and give you praise, so that I might receive
    good from you
who have already bestowed on me an existence
that is rich in all goodness.

Confessions XIII, 1

Up to Jerusalem

I beg you, O Lord,
not to leave me or remain silent;
speak truthfully to my heart
as you alone can do.
I will retreat into my room
to sing songs of love to you:
and I will weep with inexpressible sorrow
as I make my pilgrimage,
remembering Jerusalem.
My mind is turned upon you,
Jerusalem, my mother,
and turned upon you who reigns over her,
who gives her renown and are to her father,
guardian and husband,
her pure, deep delight,
her lasting joy
and the sum of all her ineffable good . . .
because you are the only
true, supreme good.
And I shall not be deflected
until you gather me up in the peace
of that most beloved mother,
where there dwell the first-fruits
of my spirit
and whence comes all my assurance;
do not gather me up
just as I am,
lost and without form,
but give me a new form and make me strong
for eternity,
O most merciful God.

Confessions XII, 16

On my mother's death

O God of my heart,
my glory and my life,
leaving aside *my mother's*
good works,
for which I gladly thank you,
now I pray to you for her sins:
hear me
through the merits of that Healer of our wounds
who was hung on a tree and
who is seated now at your right hand and
     intercedes for us.
I know that she always acted with generosity
and forgave from her heart the debts of her debtors:
will you also forgive her her sins,
if in the many years of her life after her baptism
she did anything wrong.
Forgive, O Lord,
forgive her, I beg you,
and do not put her on trial.
Mercy triumphs over judgement:
your words are truth
and you have promised mercy
to those who show mercy to others;
it is your gift that they have shown mercy
and thus you will be merciful
to those to whom you gave mercy;
you will have pity
on those to whom you showed pity.
I believe that you had already granted this
     before I asked,
but accept,
Lord,
my prayer of thanks.   *Confessions* IX, 13

Full of hope

O Lord our God,
fill us with hope
in the shadow of your wings;
protect and sustain us.
You will uphold us,
right from our childhood
until our old age:
because our present strength,
if it comes from you, is strength indeed;
but if it is merely our own strength,
then it is weakness.
When we are close to you
we find living goodness,
but at the very moment we turn aside from
    you
we become corrupt.
So, Lord, make us
retrace our steps,
so that we are not defeated;
it is only close to you
that we find our living goodness,
which is never diminished
since you yourself are goodness;
we shall not be afraid that we are no longer
in the place we fell from.
And if we do not turn aside,
we shall not fail to find
that home, that inheritance
which you have prepared for us.

Confessions IV, 16

Lord, grant us peace

O Lord my God,
   grant us your peace;
already, indeed, you have made us rich in all
   things!
Give us that peace of being at rest,
that sabbath peace,
the peace which knows no end.

PRAYING
TO GOD THE FATHER
AND CREATOR

O Lord my God, you are very great.

Psalm 104.1 NIV

Father, source of our awakening

O God,
creator of the universe,
grant that I may learn to pray;
grant that I may become worthy
of being heard by you;
grant that I may in the end be set free by you,

God,
through whom all things that would not exist
  on their own
come into being;

God, who does not let perish
things that destroy each other;

God, who created this world from nothing,
and made clear to the eyes of all
its supreme goodness;

God, who did not create evil,
but allowed it to exist
to prevent a greater evil;

God, who revealed to feeble minds
in their attempts to reach the truth
that evil has no substance;

God, thanks to whom the universe,
even when evil threatens,
is equally perfect;

God, who does not allow any dissonance

even in the most lowly things of the universe,
since the worst is in harmony with the best;

God, who is loved by all that is capable of
    loving . . .

God, who contains everything in himself
but does not accept any wickedness
from the wickedness of created beings,
nor any injury from their malice,
nor error from their errors;

God, who has given pure hearts
the gift of knowing the one true God;

O God, father of truth,
father of wisdom,
father of true life,
father of joy,
father of goodness and beauty,
father of incomprehensible light,
O father,
source of our awakening
and of our enlightenment,
who has made a pledge with us,
it is you who counsels us to return to you.

Soliloquies I, 2

By your word

How, O God, did you
create heaven and earth?
Certainly it was neither in heaven nor on the
   earth
that you made them,
nor in the air or water
which are part of
heaven and earth;
nor could you create the universe from within
   the universe,
since nowhere existed in which to do it
before it had itself been created.
You did not even hold in your hand
something from which to extract
heaven and earth,
because where could you have taken it from
if you had not already made it?
Is there anything that exists
other than because you exist?
So you gave the word
and the world was created;
you created it by your word.

Everything is a gift

O Lord,
   I thank you
that you are the most holy creator
and supreme ruler of all things.
I thank you that even if
you had not wanted me beyond my childhood
I would still have known life and feelings.
Even as a child I wanted to preserve my life,
the likeness of your most mysterious unity
from which it drew its being;
even then,
I paid heed to all my senses
and, in my modest reflections on little things,
I took pleasure in the truth.
I could not bear to be misled;
I had a good memory,
spoke well,
and was a loyal friend;
I shunned pain,
humiliation and ignorance.
In such a being,
how could anything admirable and
   praiseworthy
be lacking?
Yet all these things
are gifts from God,
I did not give them to myself:
they are good and, all together,
they make up what I am.

Thus he who made me is good,
and he is my own good:
I rejoice in his goodness

which even in childhood
filled my existence.
I thank you,
in whom I place my confidence and my trust,
I thank you, loving God,
for all your gifts,
and ask you to keep them for me.

Confessions I, 20

How great you are

O Lord my God,
   how eternally great
are your hidden depths,
and how far have the consequences of my sins
dragged me from them!
Heal my vision,
that I may rejoice with you in the light.
Indeed,
if there existed a mind so gifted
in abundant knowledge
as to know all things,
past and future,
as I know all the notes of a song,
it would be a wonderful thing,
and to be held in awe,
because nothing past or future
would be concealed from it;
just as when I sing
I know
how much I have already sung since the
   beginning
and how much remains until the end.
Nonetheless, I would be in a sorry state if I
   thought
that you, the creator of the universe,
creator of our minds and bodies,
had no more knowledge than this
of things to come and of those past!
You are far more wonderful,
far more mysterious!
For you,
who are eternal and unchanging,
the everliving creator of our minds,

it is not merely a succession of impressions
or prolonged sensations,
as for someone who sings
or listens to music.
Just as you knew heaven and earth in the
    beginning,
without any change in your knowledge,
so you created heaven and earth in the
    beginning
without any change in your action.
Whoever understands this exalts you,
but so too do those who do not understand.
How great you are!
Even the most humble
are part of your family:
you, indeed, lift those who have fallen,
and those
who place their own greatness in you
never fall.

Confessions XI, 31

71

What is God?

What is God?
I asked the earth
and it replied:
'I am not God';
and everything on earth
made the same declaration.
I asked the sea, the deep
and its living things,
and they replied:
'We are not your God.'
I asked the winds that blow,
and the whole air and its inhabitants
replied:
'I am not God.'
I asked the sky, the moon and the stars.
They replied:
'We are not the God you seek either.'
I asked everything
within me:
'Speak to me of my God;
since you are not God,
tell me something about him.'
And they cried out in a loud voice:
'It is he who made us.'
My request was born of my reflection,
and their beauty was their response.
Then I turned to myself and asked:
'Who are you?'
The reply came back:
'A man.'
I have a body and a soul at my disposal:
one is external, the other internal;
which of the two should I question about my God?

I have already sought him with my body
in the earth and sky,
using my eyes
as messengers.
Better, then, to seek him with the soul.
It was to the soul, as one who rules and
    guides,
that the messengers of the body addressed
the replies of the earth and sky
and all that is within them:
'We are not God',
'It is he who made us.'
The inner man knew these things
thanks to the outer part:
I knew then in my mind
thanks to the senses of my body . . .
You, my soul, are without doubt more
    important than my body;
I say this
because you give life to the body
and no body can do the same
to another body.
Your God, then, is the life of your life.

Confessions X, 6b

Listening

Is there anything like you, O Lord our God,
who are the unchanging Word,
never growing old
but making all things new?
If the tumult of the flesh were quiet,
if the spectres of the earth,
air and water faded away,
if the heavens were struck dumb
and if the soul itself were wrapped in silence,
rising above its self-preoccupation –
if all fell silent,
all dreams and fantasies,
every tongue, every portent and all transitory
   things,
there would remain this one proclamation:
'We did not make ourselves,
but were made by him who is everlasting.'
If, once this was said, there was silence,
because all creation were listening,
waiting for the Creator alone to speak,
not now through the things of creation,
but in his own voice,
and if we heard him speak
no longer through mortal tongue
or angel's voice or in a clap of thunder,
not in a mysterious parable,
but directly –
if he gave all things life
could be heard directly,
we would reach out
and in an instant touch Wisdom,
which reigns eternally over all things;
and it might continue like this, while other

inferior visions disappeared:
as we watched, this single vision would
   enrapture
and absorb us and fill us
with inner bliss;
eternal life
would be just like that flash of understanding
for which we have longed;
then we may answer the invitation to
'Come and share your Master's happiness'!
It will be answered
when we will not all sleep
but when we will all be changed.

Confessions IX, 10

Thank you, Lord

Thank you Lord!
We see the earth and the sky . . .
we see the light which was created and
  separated from the darkness.
We see the firmament of heaven . . .
the vast expanse of the universe . . .
and the mass of water flowing on the earth.
We see the beauty of the waters
gathered up in vast oceans . . .
and the dry earth,
first bare and then adorned,
giving birth to grass and trees.
We see the lights of heaven glowing,
the sun which is sufficient by day
and the moon and stars giving comfort by
  night . . .
We see nature's moisture
giving life to the fish, wild beasts and birds . . .
We see the face of the earth
rich in wildlife
and man made in your image and likeness,
thus having reason and intelligence
and ruling over all unintelligent life . . .
And so as we see these things
we see that they are all good,
very good.

Confessions XIII, 32

76

When I love God

In loving you,
    O Lord,
I have no feelings of doubt;
I am quite sure of it.
Your word touched my heart
and I began to love you;
see how heaven and earth
and all that is in every part of them
call to me to love you,
and . . . they call to us all,
so that there can be no excuse for not loving
    you.
You will have still greater mercy
on those you wished to pity,
and you will have compassion
on those towards whom you wished to be
    compassionate:
if it were not so,
the praises of earth and heaven would be
    falling
on deaf ears.
But what do I love in loving you?
Not physical beauty,
nor transitory charm,
nor the splendour of light
which is so dear to my eyes;
not the sweet melodies of many songs;
nor the perfume of flowers, ointments and
    spices;
not manna
nor honey;
not the delights of physical embrace.
In loving my God

I do not love such things.
Yet in loving him
I nonetheless love a certain light, a voice, a
    perfume, food
and an embrace deep within my being:
where my soul is bathed
in a light which no place can contain,
where a voice is heard
that no passage of time
can ever remove,
where a fragrance abounds
that no gust of wind can disperse,
where there is a savour
that no ravenous hunger can diminish,
where there is an embrace
that no fulfilment can bring to an end.
This is what I love
when I love my God.

Confessions X, 6

The seventh day

All this good and beautiful order
  of created things will pass away:
they have had a morning and an evening.
On the seventh day, however,
the sun will not set,
because you have blessed it,
that it might last for ever;
it is set out for us
in holy Scripture
that you wanted to rest on the seventh day,
when your perfect work was done,
although you had completed it without
    weariness;
we too, when our work is done,
even though it is good only because you accept it,
we will rest in you
in the sabbath of eternal life.
Then too you will rest in us
just as now you work in us,
and that rest will be yours through us,
just as these works now are yours through us.
You, Lord, are always at work
and ever at rest,
being neither bound by time,
nor moving nor resting in time;
yet you create what we see in time:
you create both time itself
and rest at the end of time.
So we see your completed works
because they exist;
but their reason for existing is
because you looked on them . . .
We see from outside that they exist

and understand from within that they are good,
but you saw them simultaneously made
and about to be made.
In our own time we are moved to do good
since our hearts have received
your spirit's inspiration;
previously we were moved to do evil
because we deserted you;
but you alone, O God, are good,
you have never ceased to do good.
There are some works of ours that are good
through your grace,
but they are not eternal;
yet when they are complete
we have the hope of being able to rest
in your unbounded holiness.
You who are good and rich in all goodness
are always at rest,
because you are rest itself.

Confessions XIII, 37

What are you, my God?

What are you, my God?
  Tell me what you are if not the Lord
  God?
The Lord alone is Lord,
Our God alone is God.
Most high God,
immeasurable goodness,
more than powerful,
you are all-powerful,
perfect compassion
coupled with perfect justice,
hidden from all
yet present with us all,
wholly strength and wholly beauty,
your equal is to be found only in yourself,
you are incomprehensible to man;
you who change all things cannot be changed,
never new and never old
you give new life to all things,
you bring down the proud
without their even realising it;
always active yet always at peace,
you gather all things to yourself without
  having need of them;
you support them abundantly and protect them;
you create, preserve and perfect them;
you seek although you lack nothing.
You love without the turmoil of passion,
you are solicitous and yet at peace,
you show grief but do not suffer,
you are angry and yet remain calm;
you change things without any alteration to
  your purpose

and you retrieve those you find
without ever having been without them;
you lack for nothing
but you rejoice in winning someone,
you are never avaricious yet you require some
    return;
even if we think we are giving you something
in order to put you in our debt . . .
how much do we ever possess
that does not come from you?
You pay what we are owed,
you who owe nothing to anyone:
you do not exact all that should be owed to
    you,
but lose nothing to us!
What are we to say,
my God,
my life, divine sweetness?
What remains to be said
in talking about you?
Yet woe to anyone who does not want to talk
    about you,
because otherwise he would utter useless
    nonsense.

Confessions I, 4

We believe in you, Holy Trinity

O Lord our God,
    we believe in you,
Father, Son and Holy Spirit.
For the Word would not have said:
'Go, baptise all nations
in the name of the Father and of the Son
and of the Holy Spirit,'
if you were not Trinity.
And you would not have commanded us to be
    baptised
in the name of someone who was not the Lord
    God;
nor would a voice from heaven have said:
'Hear, O Israel:
the Lord your God
is the only God',
if you were not Trinity in being,
the one Lord, the one God.
And if you were God the Father
and at the same time
the Son your Word, Jesus Christ,
and if you were your gift, the Holy Spirit,
we would not read in holy Scripture:
'God sent his Son':
nor would you, only begotten Son,
say of the Holy Spirit:
'Whom the Father will send in my name'
and again:
'He whom I will send you from the Father.'
In directing my efforts
towards this rule of faith,

it was you who enabled me to do as much as I
  could,
I sought you;
I wanted to see in my mind
what I believed,
so I have debated and laboured much.
O Lord my God, my only hope,
hear me in your goodness
and do not let me stop seeking you when I am
  weary
but let me seek your presence
ever more ardently.

On the Trinity XV, 28

PRAYING
TO GOD TO SPEAK

Lord, to whom shall we go?
You have the words of eternal life.

John 6.68 NIV

Source of joy

I call on you
O God our Truth,
who are the source, beginning and creator of
    truth
and of all that is true;
O God our Wisdom, the source, beginning
and creator of wisdom,
and of all that is wise;
God who are the true and sovereign Life,
the source, beginning and creator of life
and of all that lives
in truth and sovereignty;
O God our Blessedness,
the source, beginning and creator of joy
and of all that is joyful;
God of goodness and beauty
who is in all that is good and beautiful;
God our discernible Light,
who can be discerned in all that shines
with that light;
God whose kingdom is the whole universe
that our senses cannot perceive;
God whose kingdom lays down laws for
the kingdoms of this world;
God from whom to stray is to fall,
and to whom to return is to rise up,
in whom to remain is to rest on a firm
    foundation.

To leave you is to die,
to return to you is to come back to life,
to dwell in you is to live.

No one loses you if he does not fall into error,
no one seeks you without being called,
no one finds you without being purified.

To go away from you is to be lost, to seek you
    is to love,
to see you is to make you our own.

Faith urges us towards you,
hope guides us
and love unites us to you.

O God through whom
we triumph over the enemy,
to you I turn my prayer!

Soliloquies I, 3a

Light of the world

This is my prayer, O Lord,
giver of joy and strength,
truth of the world,
that as only you know how
you will make righteousness look down from
  heaven
and cause lights to appear in the firmament.
Let us share our food
with the hungry,
provide the poor wanderer with shelter,
clothe those who have nothing to wear,
and not turn away from our own flesh and
  blood;
such fruits spring from the earth
and you see that they are good;
so our light in this world shines out.
Through this humble harvest of action
we may delight to gaze upon
the one true Word of Life;
so let us appear as light in the world,
following you according to your holy word.
For it is in Scripture that you speak to us.

Confessions XIII, 18

I shall eat and drink

O Truth that illumines my heart,
let me not pay attention to the words of
the night!
I threw myself upon them
and found myself in darkness,
but even from those depths I loved you
greatly.
I went astray
but still remembered you.
I heard your voice behind me
telling me to turn back;
I had difficulty in hearing it
because of the restlessness
that raged within me,
but now I am returning,
thirsty and longing for your life-giving
fountain.
Let no one stop me from drawing near to it:
there I shall eat and drink.
I must not live my own life,
for on my own I lived corruptly,
on my own I was death;
but in you I came back to life.
Speak to me, instruct me.
I believe the Scriptures
but your words are full of mystery.

Confessions XII, 10

Eternal reason

Your Word is eternal reason,
present at the beginning of time yet
speaking still to us.
In the Gospel he has spoken to us in a human
voice
and opened men's ears to hear it,
that they might believe in him,
and that by seeking him within themselves
they might find eternal truth,
in which the one good Master
instructs all his followers.
There, Lord, I hear your voice telling me
that he who speaks is instructing us,
while if anyone does not instruct,
even though he speaks, it is as if he had never
spoken.
Who teaches us but that one unchanging
truth?
Even when we receive teaching
from a created being, who is subject to
change,
we are led to the unchanging truth,
where we truly learn
by waiting and listening to him
and we are full of joy when we hear the
bridegroom's voice,
restoring us to our original state.
He is the Beginning.
If while we wander in error
he did not remain constant
we would have nowhere to return to.
When we turn away from our sins
we return precisely by way of learning,

so that we might know
who it is who is teaching us,
since he is the Beginning
and talks to us now.

Confessions XI, 8

Eternal Word of God

O God, you ask us to understand the
   Word,
who is also God,
the Word spoken from eternity
by whom all things are spoken
throughout eternity.
With him one thing does not have to cease
   being said
in order for another to be heard –
everything may be spoken together throughout
   eternity . . .
I understand this, my God, and thank you for it.
I understand and proclaim it, O Lord;
anyone who is grateful for that certain truth
understands it with me and thanks you.
We know, O Lord,
that when a thing dies and is born again
it is no longer what it was
but begins to be what previously it was not.
But in your Word
there is nothing to disappear or to be
   superseded,
since it is truly immortal and eternal;
in this Word that is coeternal with you
you say everything
both in an instant and eternally:
thus everything is done
as you say it should be.
You do not act except through your Word.

Confessions XI, 7

Where did I find you?

Where did I find you
to be able to know you?
I had no innate memory of you
before I knew you;
so where did I find you to know you,
unless it was in yourself, from above?
No one place contains you:
we approach you and turn aside,
there is no one place for you.
You are Truth and sit on high
over all those who seek help from you,
and you reply simultaneously to everyone,
even though their requests are different.
You reply clearly,
but not all understand clearly.
Everyone asks you for what they want,
but they do not always
receive the reply they would like.
Your faithful servant
is not anxious to hear
what he wants from you,
so much as to desire
what he has heard you say.

Confessions X, 26

Eternal truth

Whoever knows truth
knows that light,
and whoever knows that light
knows eternity.
Love knows it.
O eternal truth,
true love, much longed for eternity!
You are my God,
I sigh to you night and day.
Hardly did I know you
than you raised me up
to make me understand that there was
    something
I could have seen
but was not yet able to see it.
Your light shone full on me,
you struck my defective vision
and I trembled with love and fear;
I realised I was far from you
in a different land,
and I seemed to hear your voice from on high:
'I am the food of the strong;
grow, and you will feed on me;
but you will not make me part of you
as you do with bodily nourishment,
but rather I will make you part of me.'

Confessions VII, 10

Happy is he who loves you

O Lord God of truth,
   is scientific learning enough
to obtain your favour?
Unhappy is he who has all knowledge
yet does not know you;
but happy is he who does know you
yet is ignorant of all else.
Anyone who has both
is not made any happier by human
   knowledge;
he is happy through you alone,
if in knowing you he honours you
and continually gives thanks for your
   greatness.

Confessions V, 4

God of the lowly

You are great, Lord,
and you care for the lowly,
while watching from afar
those who exalt themselves;
you come close only to those with contrite
  hearts,
you do not reveal yourself to the proud . . .
They use the intelligence and discernment that
  you gave them
to inquire into everything.
They have discovered much,
and have predicted eclipses of the sun and the
  moon
many years before they happened . . .
But they do not know the way
which is your Word,
through whom you created both that reality
whose dimensions they study
and the very people who measure it
and their intelligence
that enables them to measure it:
yet your wisdom is unmeasured!
Christ himself has become our wisdom,
our righteousness, holiness and redemption,
he was one of us
and paid taxes to Caesar.
These men, then, do not know how to set
  aside their arrogance
and make their way down to him,
so that through him
they may rise up to him.

Confessions V, 3

A little time for your Word

May your Scriptures be for me
a chaste joy,
that I may not make mistakes
nor mislead others with them.
Turn and have pity, O Lord my God,
you who are the light of the blind and strength
   of the weak,
the light of those who do see and the strength
   of those who are strong,
turn to my soul and listen
when it calls from the depths.
If your ears were not present
to hear us from the depths,
where should we go?
To whom should we cry?
The day is yours and yours too is the night,
time passes at your bidding.
Grant me a little of that time
for my meditations
on the mysteries of your Word,
do not close the door to those who knock.
It was not without purpose that you willed
so many pages of deep mystery to be written:
but those dark forests nonetheless have their deer
who seek refuge and refreshment there,
wandering and grazing,
lying down and pondering.
Lord, complete your work in me
and make those pages clear to me.
For me your voice is a joy
greater than any other.
Grant me what I love
because I love,

and grant me too that same love.
Do not withhold your gifts
nor neglect this parched grass.
Let me honour you
for all that I have found in your Books,
let me listen to the sound of your praise,
let me quench my thirst from you
and contemplate the wonders of your Word,
from the beginning when you created heaven
    and earth,
until the time when we reign with you
in eternity in your holy city.

Lord have pity on me
and grant what I desire.
I do not believe that this is a desire for earthly
    things,
for gold, silver or precious stones,
fine clothes, honour and power,
sensual pleasures
or things needed for the body
or for this life of pilgrimage.
All these things will be given to us as well
if we seek your kingdom and its justice.
You see, my God,
whence my longing springs.
The godless have told me what they covet,
which is not in obedience to your law,
O Lord.
But my longing is inspired by that law.
Look, Father, look at me,
look and approve,
and may it be pleasing to you in your mercy
that I should find favour with you,
so that the hidden meanings of your words
might be revealed to me, because I knock.

I make my plea to you
through our Lord Jesus Christ,
the Son of Man at your right hand,
whom you have set as a mediator between
    yourself and us,
through him
you came to seek us
who did not seek you,
and you sought us
so that we too might seek you;
your Word
through whom you made all things,
myself among them,
your only Son,
through whom you have called by adoption
a people of believers,
and myself among them.
I entreat you in the name of him
who sits at your right hand and intercedes for us,
in whom are hidden all the treasures
of wisdom and knowledge.
These are what I seek in your books,
He is the one of whom Moses wrote,
and he himself says it,
he is Truth.

Confessions XI, 2

Help me to understand

Help me to hear and understand
how in the beginning you created
heaven and earth.
Moses wrote of this,
he wrote it down and then he fell asleep,
passing out of this world to you,
so I cannot have him in front of me now.
If he were here I would catch hold of him
and ask him questions . . .
Since I cannot question Moses
I turn to you,
who are the Truth, with whom he was filled
in speaking his words of truth;
I beg you, my God,
forgive my sins,
and as you have allowed your servant
to speak these words,
so help me to understand them.

Set me free from useless words

Set me free, O God,
from the abundance of words from which
   I suffer
deep within my soul,
which is unhappy in your sight
and takes refuge in your mercy.
Indeed, even when my lips are silent
my thoughts are not.
If I could at least think of something
pleasing to you,
then I certainly would not beg you
to set me free
from this surfeit of words.
But my thoughts are many,
and you know that the thoughts of men
are vain.
Help me not to give in to them
and if ever they delight me
grant that I may disapprove of them
and do not abandon me to them
as if to a kind of sleep.
Let them not ever have such power over me
as to influence all my actions,
and that with your protection
my consciousness and discernment
may be free from their influence . . .
When we arrive in your presence
there will be an end to the many words we utter
that do not reach you:
you will remain, one alone,
yet in all things,

and when we become one in you
for all eternity,
we will utter just one word
to praise you in a single burst of sound.
O Lord,
one God,
God the holy Trinity,
let your people know that
all I have written in these books
is of you;
and if there is anything of me in them,
forgive me,
and may your people forgive me.
Amen.

On the Trinity XV, 28

PRAYING
TO GOD THE SOURCE
OF ALL GIFTS

Praise the Lord, O my soul.

Psalm 103.1 NIV

I praise and thank you

I thank you, O my light,
that you have lit my way
and I have known you.
How have I known you?
I have known you as the only true and living
   God,
my creator.
I have known you
as the creator of heaven and earth
and of all things seen and unseen,
almighty God, true, immortal, invisible,
unmeasured and unbounded,
eternal and inaccessible;
incomprehensible, immense and infinite;
the beginning of all creatures
seen and unseen,
by whom all the elements
are created and sustained . . .
I have known you as the one unique, true and
   eternal God:
Father, Son and Holy Spirit,
three persons but one single essence,
one indivisible nature of perfect simplicity.
I have learnt that the Father proceeds from no
   one
and that only the Son proceeds from the
   Father
and the Spirit from them both,
without beginning,
and ever without end,
one and triune God,
unique cause of all things
visible and invisible,

spiritual and bodily . . .
I have come to know you and I praise you
God, the Father, not begotten
you, the only begotten Son,
and you, Spirit, Holy Paraclete,
neither generate nor ingenerate,
holy and single Trinity in three
coequal, consubstantial, coeternal Persons,
Trinity in unity,
unity in Trinity.
I believe with my heart as is just,
and praise you with my lips in the hope of
    salvation.

My joy, my reason, my dwelling

You are everything,
  you are as much as I have said in my
  prayer.
Come to my help,
one true and eternal substance;
in you there is no discord,
no confusion, no change,
no defect, no death;
in you there reigns total harmony,
total clarity and constancy,
total fullness and life;
in you there is neither too little
nor too much;
with you
He who created and he who was begotten
are one and the same.
All things serve you
and every good soul is obedient to you.
Your laws govern the movement of the earth
and fix the course of the stars:
they give the heat of the sun by day
and the gentle light of the moon by night,
guarding the balance of the universe
and giving all created matter its form.
From you all good things are poured out for us
and you put far from us all that is evil.
There is nothing above you,
nothing beyond you,
nothing without you.
Everything is in submission to you
and everything is contained in you,

everything revolves round you.
You created man
in your own image and likeness
as everyone who knows himself acknowledges:
hear me.
Hear me, O God,
my Lord, my King and my Father.
You are my first cause,
my hope,
my joy, my reason and my dwelling,
my light and my salvation,
my life!
Hear me
as only you are able,
as few men will know.

Soliloquies I, 4

Sons of light

In the morning I will arise and make my
  prayer;
I will always praise him;
in the morning I will arise
and I will see my salvation,
my God,
who will yet give life to our mortal bodies
through the Spirit who dwells in us,
who moves in his mercy
over our inner being,
as over dark waters:
we have this promise
on our pilgrimage,
that we shall walk in the light,
and now we are saved by hope,
we are sons of light and sons of the day,
and no longer the sons of the night and of
  darkness
which we were before.
In the still uncertain knowledge of men
you alone can distinguish those in darkness
  and those in the light,
you who test our hearts
and who called the light day and the darkness
  night.
Who indeed can tell us apart, if not you?
What do we have that is not your gift?

Confessions XIII, 14b

111

By your grace, O God, we do not suffer total death

By your grace, O God,
we do not suffer total death.
You warn us to be watchful.
By your grace
we distinguish good from evil
we can shun evil and seek good
and not fall into adversity.
By your grace
we are enabled both to command and obey.
By your grace
we discover that sometimes
what we think is ours is alien to us
and what we think is alien is ours.
By your grace
we are freed from the snares and attacks of evil.
It is through you
that little things do not make us small.
By you
the best in us
is not suffocated
by the worst in us.
By you
death is swallowed up in victory.
God, you lead us to yourself
and divest us of what exists no more
in order to clothe us in what does exist.
God, you make us worthy to be heard by you.
You strengthen us
and make us know all truth.
You offer us that good
which stops us from becoming fools

and you do not allow others to make us foolish.
You lead us back onto the right path.
You take us right up to the door
and open it wide to those who knock.
You give us the bread of life
and by your grace
we drink of the water
which takes away all thirst.
You convict the world of sin
of justice and of judgement.
By your grace
we are not troubled by those who do not
    believe . . .
By you
we are not slaves
to weakness and disease.
O God,
who purifies and prepares us for divine rewards,
come to me in your favour.

Happiness and truth

Happiness is the possession of truth
and truth is rejoicing in you,
O Lord my light,
my salvation,
my God.
This happiness,
this life, the only happy life,
is desired by all:
everyone longs
to possess the truth.

Confessions X, 23

You are happiness

O Lord, take away the idea
     from the mind of your servant
who confesses to you,
that any joy whatsoever is happiness.
There is one joy that is not granted to the wicked,
but only to those who give you honour
without expecting any reward;
for them you yourself are joy.
This indeed is happiness:
rejoicing in you,
about you,
for you;
this and nothing else.
Whoever believes that there is happiness other
     than in you
is pursuing something different,
not the possession of true happiness.

Confessions X, 22

Make your dwelling in the Word

Do not be foolish, O my soul;
do not deafen my heart
with the noise of your vanities.
Take heed instead:
the Word himself is calling you back.
In him there is unending peace
whenever love is not withheld,
unless it is withheld from the Word himself.
In this world, however, all things pass away
and are not replaced . . .
But the Word of God asks:
'Do I too disappear?'
So make your dwelling in him,
O my soul,
entrust him with all that you receive from him,
tired as you are, now, of being deceived!
Entrust to the Truth all that he gives you
and you will lose nothing;
all that is corrupt in you will flourish again,
all your sickness will be healed,
all your weakness will be strengthened,
and you will be restored and renewed;
you will no longer be dragged downwards
but you will remain upright
before God,
who is all powerful and unchanging.

Confessions IV, 11

Thanksgiving for my mother

Accept my confession and my gratitude
O God,
for all the things I keep silent about.
But I will leave out nothing
my soul can produce
concerning your servant who gave birth to me
both in the flesh,
when I was born into the light of this world,
and in spirit,
when I was born into eternal light.
I will not speak of her own qualities
but of the gifts that you gave her;
because she was not her own maker,
nor her own teacher:
it was you who made her, and
neither her father nor her mother could foresee
the personality of the child they had
        produced.
It was through the guidance of Christ,
the discipline of your only son,
that she learned to hold you in awe,
in a family of believers
and as a good member of your church . . .
My mother served all your servants.
Whoever came to know her
felt gratitude,
honour, and deep love for you,
because they sensed your presence in her,
a testimony to the fruits of her holy life.
She was the wife of one man,
she fulfilled all her duties to her parents
and ordered her home with devotion,
her good works were her testimony;

she raised sons
and felt again the pangs of labour
whenever she saw them moving away from you.
Finally, O Lord,
(and if your servant has any gift of speech it
    comes from you)
before she fell asleep for ever,
when we were already living in community,
having received the grace of your baptism,
she took care of us
as if she had been mother to us all,
and served us
as if she had been the daughter of each one of us.

Confessions IX, 8–9

Happy is he who loves you and loves his friend in you

Happy is he who loves you
and loves his friend in you,
and loves his enemy in your name!
It is surely he alone
who never loses a dear one
because all are dear to him,
through him who is never lost,
through our God;
God who created heaven and earth
fills them with his presence,
just as he created them
by filling them with himself.
No one can lose you
if he does not go away from you;
and if he does go away from you,
where will he go,
where will he escape, far from your goodness,
except to run into your anger?
And then in his anguish
he will find your Word,
your Word which is truth,
and the truth is you.

Writing the truth

O Lord my God,
if I am complaining in the midst of these
people,
among Christ's family,
among your poor,
it is because I want to be able to satisfy with
your bread
those men
who do not hunger and thirst for righteousness
but who are satiated
and have plenty.
Yet they are full of their own imaginings
and not filled with the truth that they spurn
and run away from,
only to fall into their own vanity.
I know from experience what deceits
are generated by the human heart:
and what is my heart
if not a human one?
That is why I pray to God from my heart that
I should not write any such deceits
in place of the firm truth:
but rather
that my poor strength might bear some fruit
– although I am so far
from your sight,
so far that I force myself back to the path
traced by your only son
in his humanity and divinity –
and I pray that this fruit may come from that place
whence blows on me
the gentle wind of your Son's truth.
That Truth pleases me all the more

since I who am liable to change
can perceive nothing changeable in it,
no change caused by time or space,
as our bodies suffer . . .
God is eternal truth,
eternal love;
love is true,
eternity is true;
truth is loved,
as is eternity.

On the Trinity IV, Proemio

Sources

Commentary on the Psalms
Soliloquies
On the Trinity
Confessions
Book of the Soul's Soliloquies with God[1]

[1]Quasten's authoritative study classifies this work among those attributed to Augustine, but its authenticity is not fully established. Cf Quasten, *Patrologia* III, Turin, 1978.